This book belongs to ...

....

OXFORD
UNIVERSITY PRESS

Great Clarendon Street, Oxford, OX2 6DP, United Kingdom

Oxford University Press is a department of the University of Oxford.
It furthers the University's objective of excellence in research, scholarship and
education by publishing worldwide. Oxford is a registered trade mark of Oxford
University Press in the UK and in certain other countries

How the Bear Lost His Tail Text © Susan Price 2011
Illustrations © Sara Ogilvie
The Frog Prince Text © Oxford University Press 2011
Illustrations © Yannick Robert
Monkey's Magic Pipe Text © Pam Thomson 2011
Illustrations © Alessandra Cimatoribus
Yoshi the Stonecutter Text © Becca Heddle 2011
Illustrations © Meg Hunt

The moral rights of the authors have been asserted

How the Bear Lost His Tail, The Frog Prince, Monkey's Magic Pipe, Yoshi the Stonecutter
first published in 2011

This Edition published in 2014

British Library Cataloguing in Publication Data
Data available

ISBN: 978-0-19-273608-6

10 9 8 7 6 5 4 3 2

Typeset in Plantin Infant

Printed in China

Paper used in the production of this book is a natural, recyclable product
made from wood grown in sustainable forests. The manufacturing process
conforms to the environmental regulations of the country of origin.

Acknowledgements

Series Advisor: Nikki Gamble

Helping your child's learning
with free eBooks, essential
tips and fun activities
www.oxfordowl.co.uk

Traditional Tales

How the Bear Lost His Tail

and Other Stories

OXFORD

UNIVERSITY PRESS

Tips for reading How the Bear Lost His Tail together

About the story

This story is known in many cultures, including Norse and North American. It belongs to the tradition that explains why some things in the world are as they are.

This book revises sounds your child should already be familiar with. However, they might find these words tricky:

**grumpy   caught   either   icicle
laughing   believe**

Say these words for your child if they do not know them.

- Before you begin, ask your child to read the title to you by sounding out and blending. Talk about what the story might be about. How do they think the bear might have lost his tail?

- Encourage your child to read the story to you. Talk about the pictures as you read.

- Your child will be able to read most of the words in the story, but if they struggle with a word, remind them to say the sounds in the word from left to right. Ask them to point to the sounds as they say them, and then blend the sounds into a whole word, e.g. b-ear.

- Encourage your child to use lots of expression as they read. Draw attention to punctuation that adds expression to the story as it is read aloud, such as exclamation marks, commas, speech marks and question marks.

- After you have read the story, look through it again and talk about it. What kind of character do they think Fox is?

- Do the 'Retell the story' activity together!

How the Bear Lost His Tail

Written by Susan Price

Illustrated by Sara Ogilvie

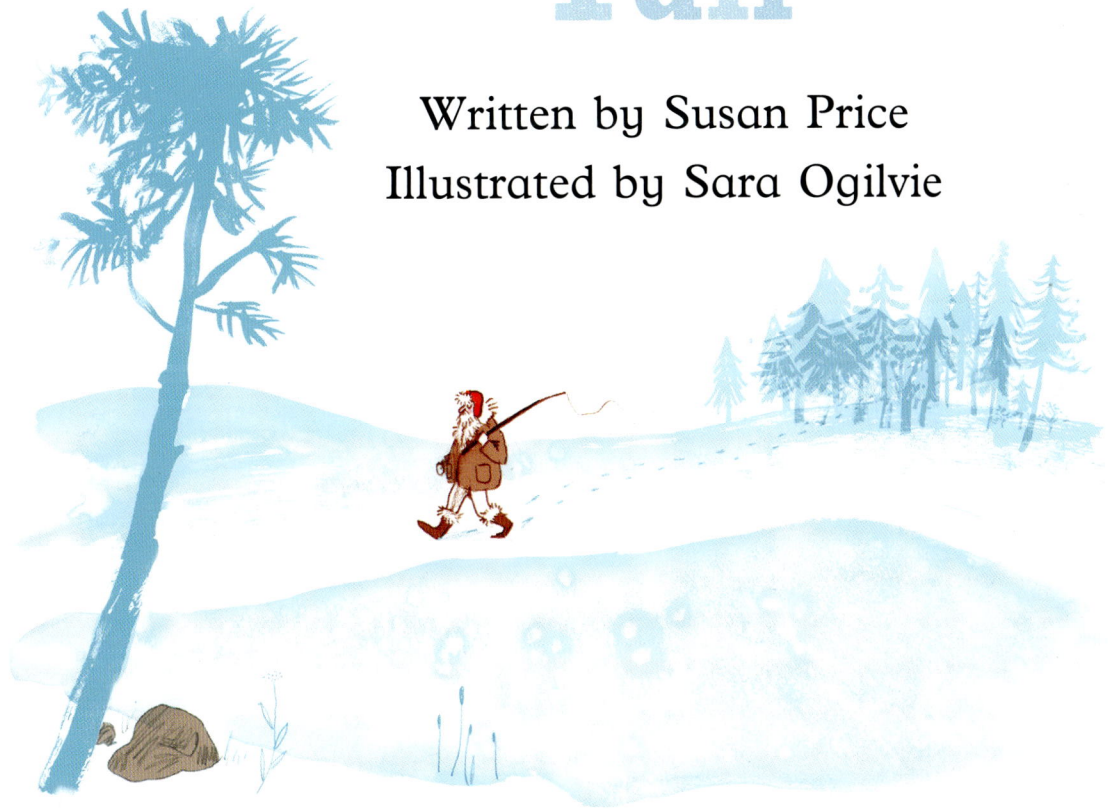

OXFORD
UNIVERSITY PRESS

We all know how bears are, don't we?

Bears are big, hairy and grumpy, with short, stumpy tails.

Bears weren't always like that though.

Once, long ago, bears were different.

They were still big and hairy, but they were sweet and kind, and had long, fluffy tails. Bears were proud of their tails in those days.

How did the bear get a stumpy tail?
Why are they so grumpy now?
Fox is to blame.

Let me tell you what Fox did.

Fox was trotting about one cold day, looking for something to eat.

He saw a fisherman by a frozen lake, dangling a line through a hole in the ice.

The fisherman had caught a lot of fish. They were lying in the snow, tied together with string. Fox was hungry.

Fox was sly and quick. He sneaked up, grabbed the string of fish, and ran as fast as he could!

In the forest, he met Bear. Bear was hungry too. He waved his long, fluffy tail and said, "Oh, Fox! Where did you get all those fish from?"

Fox saw that Bear's tail was even longer and fluffier than his.

Fox did not like that one bit. He did not want to share his fish either.

So Fox said, "I caught them!"

"How?" asked Bear.

"All you have to do is break a hole in the ice on the lake," said Fox. "Then sit down and put your tail in the water."

"It will be cold!" said Bear.
"Yes, but you will catch
a lot of fish! Sit still, and the
fish will come and nibble
your tail," said Fox.

"It might hurt, but don't pull your tail
out, or you will lose the fish! Your tail is so
long, you will catch even more than I did!"

"Oh, thank you, Fox!" said Bear. "Remember, don't pull your tail out too soon!" Fox said…

…and he ran on, with his stolen fish.

Bear went down to the frozen lake. He did everything Fox had said. He broke a hole in the ice, and put his long, fluffy tail in the icy water.

It tingled. The water was cold! The tingling got worse as the fish began to bite. But Bear kept his tail in the water, just as Fox had said to do.

Ouch!

The water in the lake was so cold, the hole behind
Bear began to freeze over again.
But Bear did not see.

Bear had to grit his teeth. The more it tingled,
the more fish he thought he was catching.

But soon it was too much for Bear.

"I don't care if I lose my fish. This hurts too much!" he thought.

He tried to pull his tail out of the water.

But his tail had frozen! It snapped off like an icicle, leaving nothing but a stump. He did not even have any fish.

Fox had made a fool of him.

From that day to this,
all bears have had short,
stumpy tails.

They are grumpy because
they think everyone is
laughing at them.

And Fox? Fox is still as quick and sly
and clever as ever.

Bear, on the other hand, has learned that he shouldn't believe everything he is told.

Encourage your child to retell the story in their own words using the pictures as prompts. You could do this together, or take it in turns. Have fun!

Once upon a time...

The end.

Tips for reading The Frog Prince together

About the story

This story is based on a tale that was first written by the Brothers Grimm about two hundred years ago.

This book revises sounds your child should already be familiar with. However, they might find these words tricky:

talk   friend   easy

Say these words for your child if they do not know them.

- Before you begin, ask your child to read the title to you by sounding out and blending. Talk about what the story might be about. What do they think might happen to the Frog Prince?

- Encourage your child to read the story to you. Talk about the pictures as you read.

- Your child will be able to read most of the words in the story, but if they struggle with a word, remind them to say the sounds in the word from left to right. Ask them to point to the sounds as they say them, and then blend the sounds into a whole word, e.g. p-o-n-d.

- Encourage your child to use lots of expression as they read. Draw attention to punctuation that adds expression to the story as it is read aloud, such as exclamation marks, commas, speech marks and question marks.

- After you have read the story, look through it again and talk about it. What do they think the Princess learned from Frog?

- Do the 'Retell the story' activity together!

The Frog Prince

Written by Pippa Goodhart

Illustrated by Yannick Robert

OXFORD
UNIVERSITY PRESS

Long ago and far away, there lived a princess. On her birthday the Queen said, "I promise to give you any toy you want."

"I want a ball made of gold," said the Princess.

"There are no balls made of gold," said the Queen.

"But a promise is a promise," said the Princess.

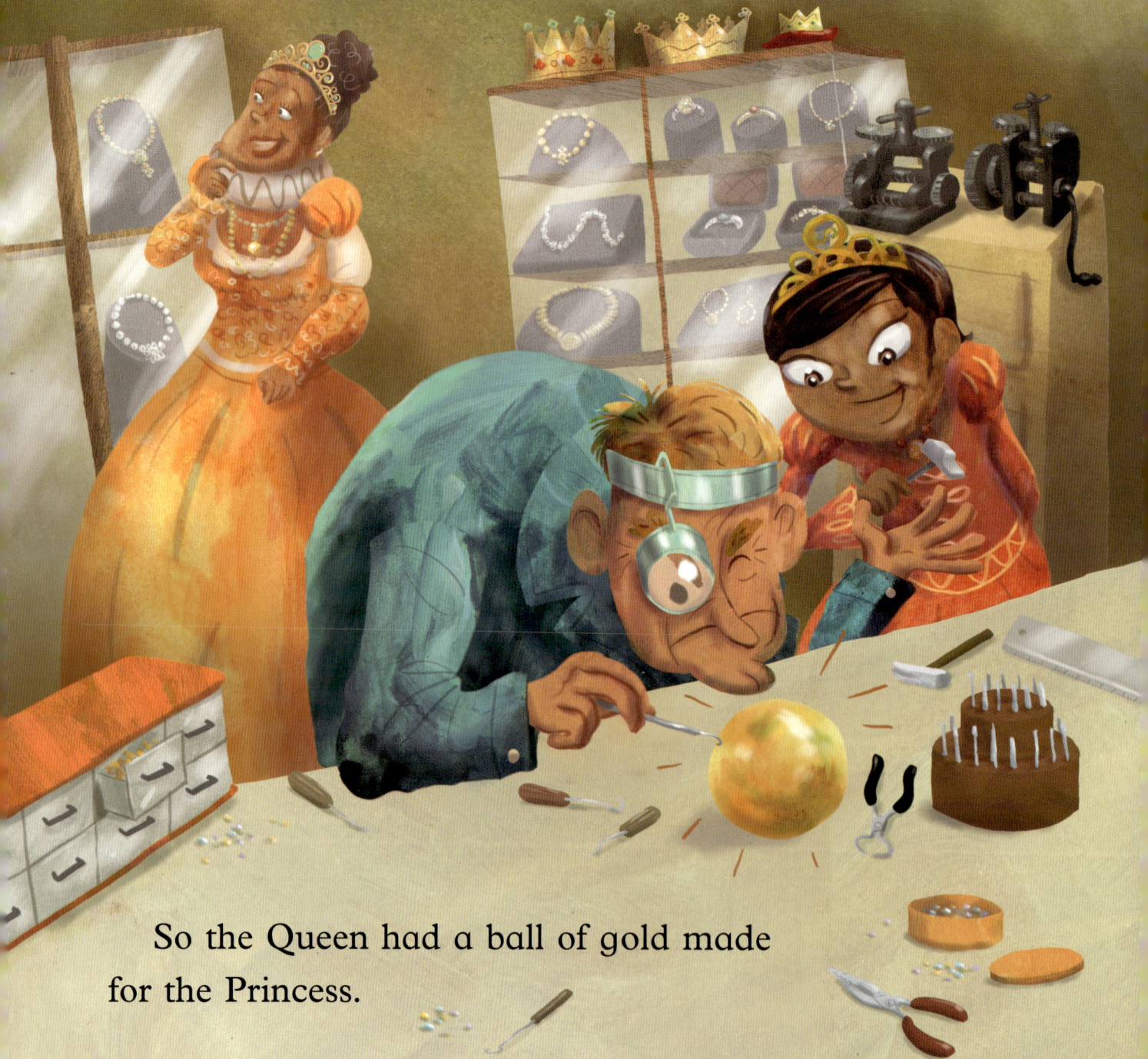

So the Queen had a ball of gold made
for the Princess.

One day the Princess was playing with her ball.
But the ball fell into the pond.

"I have lost my ball made of gold!" said the Princess.
She began to cry.

A small frog hopped over to the Princess.
"I can get your ball back," the frog said.
"Frogs can't talk!" said the Princess.

"Well I can!" said Frog.

"I will get your ball back," said Frog. "But only if you make me a promise."

"I will promise anything you like," said the Princess. "You can even have my crown!"

"A frog has no need for a crown," said Frog.

"What *do* you want, then?" said the Princess.

"I want you to promise to be my friend," said Frog.

"Easy!" said the Princess. "I will do that."

So Frog jumped into the pond. He got the ball back, just as he had promised.

"Now we will be friends," he said.

Splash!

The Princess grabbed the ball. She did not say 'thank you' to Frog.

"Hey!" said Frog. "What about your promise?"
But the Princess just ran away.

Later, as the Princess ate her supper, she heard
a sound.

"What's that?" said the Queen.

"Nothing," said the Princess.

"Open the door!" said the Queen.
"No, please don't!" said the Princess.

The Queen opened the door.
"Oh no!" said the Princess.

Frog came into the room.
"Good evening," he said.

"What do you want, Frog?" said the Queen.

"I want the Princess to be my friend, just as she promised," said Frog.

"I can't be friends with a cold, wet frog!"
said the Princess.

"A promise is a promise," said the Queen.

So Frog sat at the table and ate supper from a plate made of gold.

Slurp!

Burp!

"Now will you go back to the pond?"
said the Princess.

"A real friend would let me stay," said Frog.
"A promise is a promise."

So the Princess took Frog up to her bedroom.

"You can sleep in this nice box," said the Princess.

"A real friend would let me sleep on her pillow," said Frog.

So the Princess put Frog on her pillow.

As he sat on the pillow, magic happened.
Frog grew and grew. He changed into … a boy!
"Who *are* you?" said the Princess.

Boing!

"I am a prince," said the boy. "A witch turned me into a frog. The only thing that could turn me back into a prince was somebody being a good friend to me."

"But I was a bad friend," said the Princess. "I didn't like you at first."

"You were a good friend," said the Prince. "You gave me food. You even let me sit on your pillow."

The Princess and the Prince became
real friends. They liked to play with the
ball made of gold, but they never went
near the pond.

When they grew up, the Prince and Princess
got married.

They promised to love each other for ever.
And they did love each other for ever and ever.
After all, a promise is a promise.

Encourage your child to retell the story in their own words using the pictures as prompts. You could do this together, or take it in turns. Have fun!

Once upon a time...

56

The end.

Tips for reading Monkey's Magic Pipe together

About the story

This story is based on a South American tale where the smallest, weakest creature triumphs.

This book revises sounds your child should already be familiar with. However, they might find these words tricky:

**huge   horrible   beware   flew
panther   tune**

Say these words for your child if they do not know them.

- Before you begin, ask your child to read the title to you by sounding out and blending. Talk about what the story might be about. What might be magic about Monkey's pipe?

- Encourage your child to read the story to you. Talk about the pictures as you read.

- Your child will be able to read most of the words in the story, but if they struggle with a word, remind them to say the sounds in the word from left to right. Ask them to point to the sounds as they say them, and then blend the sounds into a whole word, e.g. g-r-a-bb-ed.

- Encourage your child to use lots of expression as they read. Draw attention to punctuation that adds expression to the story as it is read aloud, such as exclamation marks, commas, speech marks and question marks.

- After you have read the story, look through it again and talk about it. Why do they think Monster fell for Monkey's trick so easily?

- Do the 'Retell the story' activity together!

Monkey's Magic Pipe

Written by Pat Thomson

Illustrated by Alessandra Cimatoribus

OXFORD
UNIVERSITY PRESS

Long ago, in a faraway forest, lived a monster.
He lived in a cave of bones.

He was huge.

He was hairy.

He was hungry.

One morning, the Monster went into the forest with
his hunting bag.

He sang in his horrible voice,
"I'm going to eat you. Wait and see.
I'm the Monster. Beware of me!"

Snake slid away.
Parrot flew off.
Panther hid.

The Monster went to the
drinking pool.

He sat and waited.

He had hairy arms for catching.

He had big, yellow teeth for crunching.

"I am the best at waiting," he said.

As he sat in a bush by the pool,
he sang in his horrible voice,
    "I'm going to eat you. Wait and see.
    I'm the Monster. Beware of me!"

Snake was first to come to drink.

As she slid into the pool, the Monster pounced.

"Got you!" shouted the Monster. "Into my bag."
Snake was trapped.

Parrot was next to come to the pool.

As he flew down, the Monster grabbed him.

"Got you!" shouted the Monster. "Into my bag."

Parrot was trapped.

Then Panther slipped out of the shadows.

He was strong, but the Monster was stronger.

"Got you!" shouted the Monster. "Into my bag."
Even Panther was trapped.

"I shall eat them all," roared the Monster,
as he set off back to his cave of bones.
The bag bumped along behind him.
"I am the best at hunting!" he said.

The Monster saw Monkey
sitting under a tree.

"Yum," he said. "Pudding!"

Monkey had a pipe in her
little paw. She looked at the
hunting bag.

Monkey knew her friends were
inside, but she was clever and
had an idea to set them free.
"Monster," she called, "you
are the best dancer in the forest.
This new tune is just for you."

"I must be the best dancer,"
said the Monster, "because I am
the best at everything."
He pointed his hairy toe.
"Play for me," he said.

Monkey played and the Monster danced.
Then Monkey stopped.

"It's no good," she said sadly.
"What a pity. You dance so well."

"What do you mean?" roared the Monster.
"You need a partner," said Monkey.

"I have one," said the Monster, and dragged
Snake out of his bag.

The Monster put Snake around his neck and danced and danced.

"Good," said Monkey. "Now change partners."

The Monster opened his bag again and took out Parrot.
Snake slid away.

Parrot just flapped and screeched. He was not a good dancer.

The Monster had to dance around him.

"I am the best at dancing," the Monster said.

"Change partners," called Monkey.
The Monster opened his bag again.
He pulled Panther out by his tail.

Parrot flew off.

Panther struggled and snapped.

The Monster danced faster and faster.

He stamped his hairy feet and clicked his claws.

"Change partners," called Monkey.

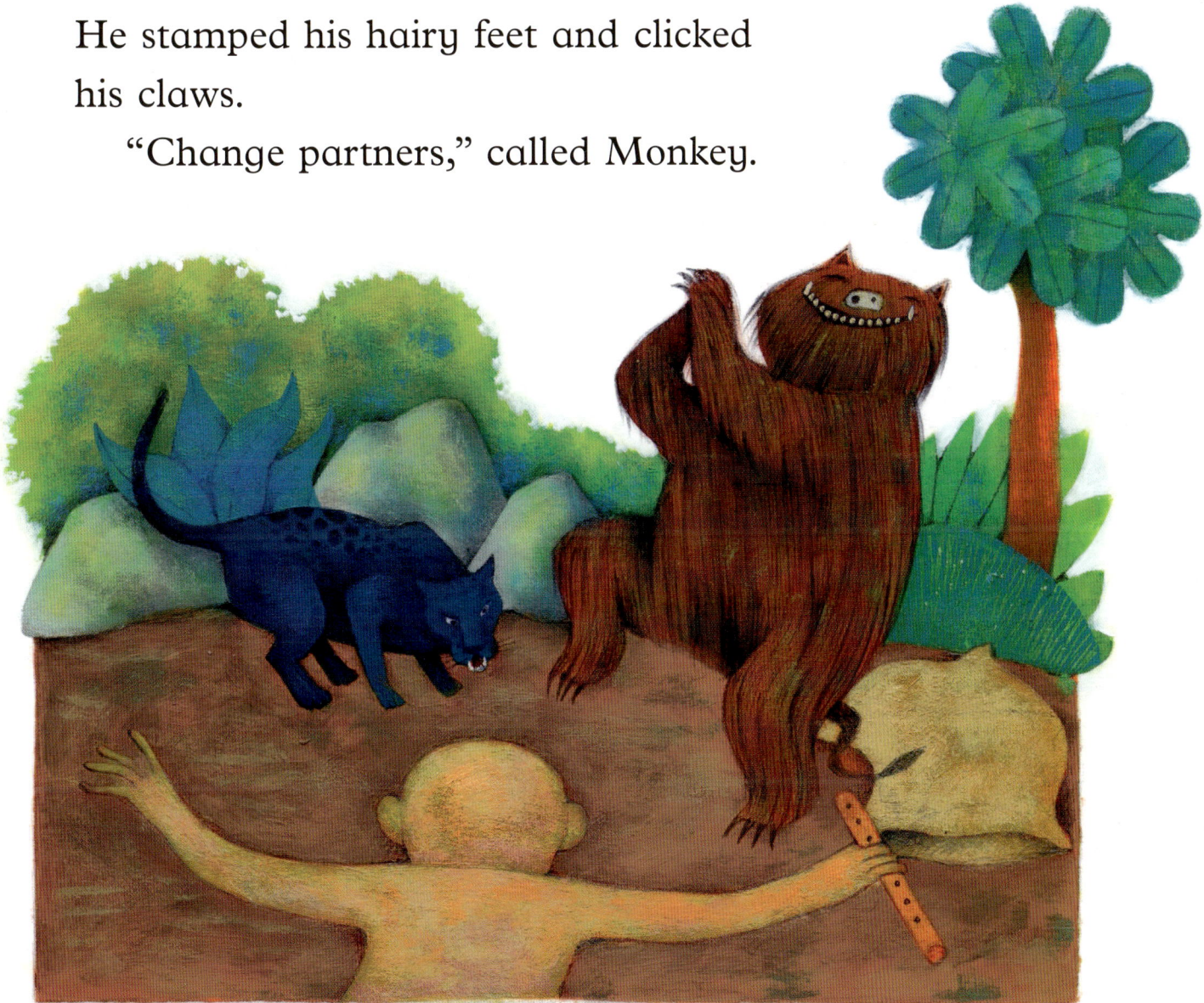

Panther sprang into the bushes.
The Monster looked in his hunting bag.

"My bag is empty," he roared.
The leaves shook on every tree.

The Monster chased Monkey,
puffing and panting.

But he was so tired he could hardly
sing his song...

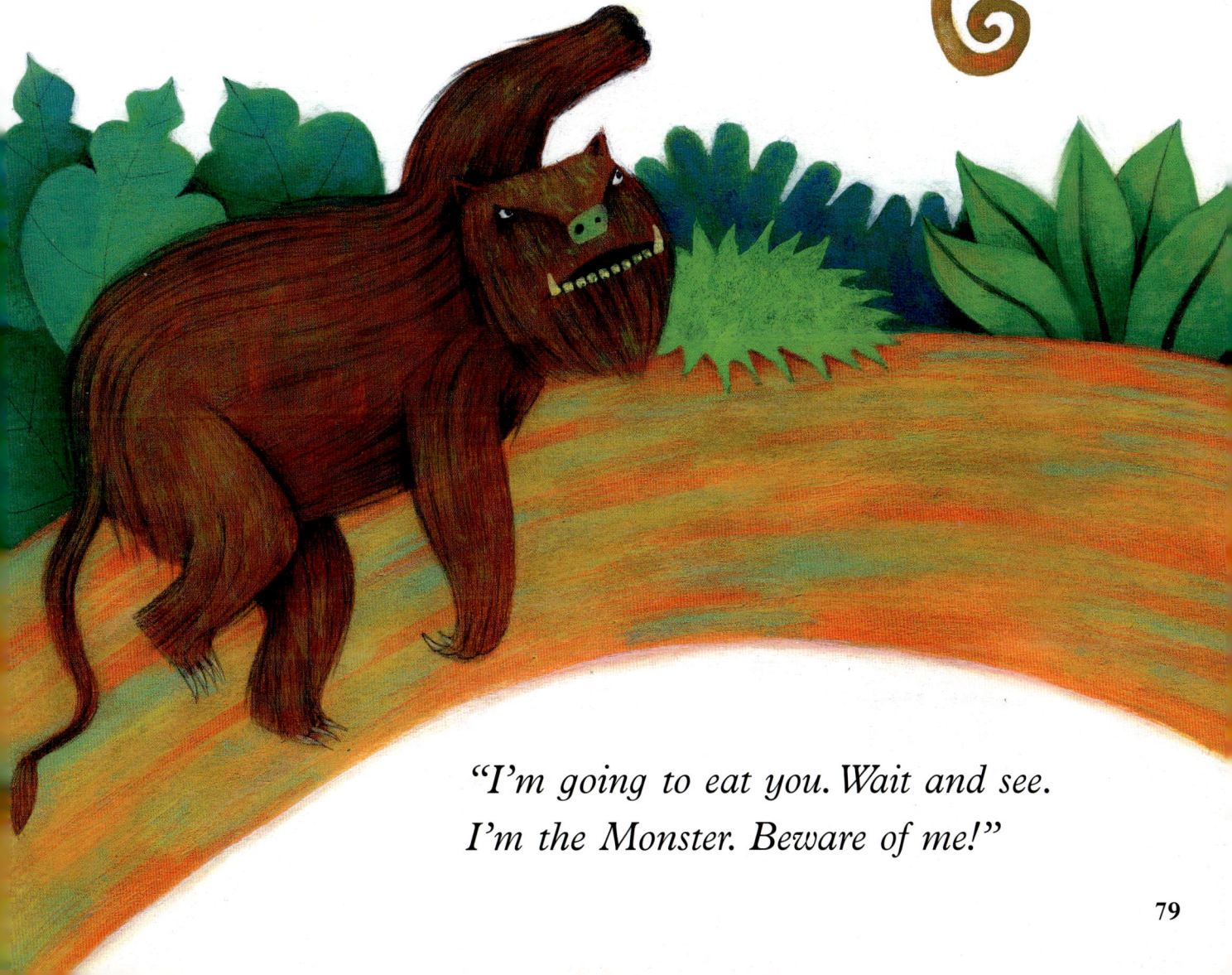

"*I'm going to eat you. Wait and see.
I'm the Monster. Beware of me!*"

"Not today," said Monkey.
"Today, Monkey is the best of all!"

Monkey skipped away, playing her pipe.
And all the animals who heard it danced.

And what happened to the Monster?

He was so tired, he lay down in his cave of bones
and snored until the bones rattled.

If you ever find his cave...

Don't go in!

Encourage your child to retell the story in their own words using the pictures as prompts. You could do this together, or take it in turns. Have fun!

Once upon a time...

The end.

Tips for reading Yoshi the Stonecutter together

About the story

This Japanese story shows how wanting more than we have is not always a good thing.

This book revises sounds your child should already be familiar with. However, they might find these words tricky:

spirit   clothes   whispered   shaded carriage   sweat

Say these words for your child if they do not know them.

- Before you begin, ask your child to read the title to you by sounding out and blending. Talk about what the story might be about. Do they think it would be easy or hard to be a stonecutter? Why?

- Encourage your child to read the story to you. Talk about the pictures as you read.

- Your child will be able to read most of the words in the story, but if they struggle with a word, remind them to say the sounds in the word from left to right. Ask them to point to the sounds as they say them, and then blend the sounds into a whole word, e.g. r-i-v-er-s.

- Encourage your child to use lots of expression as they read. Draw attention to punctuation that adds expression to the story as it is read aloud, such as exclamation marks, commas, speech marks and question marks.

- After you have read the story, look through it again and talk about it. Do they think Yoshi was greedy? Why?

- Do the 'Retell the story' activity together!

Yoshi
the Stonecutter

Written by Becca Heddle

Illustrated by Meg Hunt

OXFORD

UNIVERSITY PRESS

Long ago in the mountains of Japan, there lived a stonecutter called Yoshi. He was a poor man with a bent back and hard hands from cutting stone.

People said a spirit lived in the
mountains where Yoshi worked.
They said it granted wishes.

But Yoshi had never seen the
spirit.

One day, Yoshi took some stone to a rich man's house. Yoshi loved the rich man's beautiful home, his silk clothes and his clean, soft hands.

"Oh, I wish I could be a rich man," whispered Yoshi. A cool wind blew and the mountain spirit appeared. It whispered, "Your wish is granted, Yoshi – a rich man you now shall be."

When Yoshi got home, his hut
had become a fine house.

Yoshi was rich. He put away his tools
and rested, looking out of the window.

The day grew hot. Yoshi saw a prince ride by.
Servants fanned the prince to cool him, and shaded
him with golden umbrellas.

"I wish I could be a prince," said Yoshi.

The spirit said, "Your wish is granted, Yoshi – a prince you now shall be."

Now Yoshi was a prince, riding in a carriage with servants around him.

Prince Yoshi smiled as he sheltered from the sun under golden umbrellas. His servant gave him water in a jewelled cup and Yoshi happily sipped it.

Prince Yoshi soon felt very hot – even the umbrellas didn't help.

When he splashed water on his skin, the hot sun soon dried it up.

"The sun is more powerful than me," muttered Yoshi. "I wish I could be the sun."

The spirit spoke again. "Your wish is granted, Yoshi – the sun you now shall be."

Yoshi felt himself rise into the sky and start to shine. He really was the sun! He sent his powerful rays down to Earth.

Yoshi shone harder. He made people sweat and burned their skin. He dried out the land and made the grass wither. Everything could feel his power.

One day, Yoshi the sun could not see the ground. A cloud was in his way. He shone with all his might, but the cloud would not go.

"Can a cloud blot out my power?" cried Yoshi. "Then I wish I could be a cloud."

"Your wish is granted, Yoshi – a cloud you now shall be," replied the spirit.

Yoshi became a big, thick grey cloud. He shut out the sun's heat and shaded the people. He cooled the land, and then he began to rain.

Yoshi's rain made streams and rivers flow, and made puddles on the ground. The grass soon turned green again and the crops began to grow.

Yoshi the cloud rained harder and harder. In the mountains, the little streams became great waterfalls. Rivers overflowed and drowned the crops.

The flood water came rushing down roads and poured into villages. Only the huge rocks on the mountains stood firm and would not move.

"Rocks are more powerful than clouds," grumbled Yoshi. "I wish I could be a rock."

The spirit replied, "Your wish is granted, Yoshi – a rock you now shall be."

Now Yoshi was a rock – huge, hard and solid.

He did not fear the sun or the rain.

"Nothing can be stronger than me," he boasted.

Then Yoshi the rock felt tools cutting into him.

"A stonecutter is stronger than me!" said Yoshi.
"I wish I could be a man again."

The mountain spirit smiled. "Your wish is granted,
Yoshi – a man you now shall be."

Yoshi the stonecutter picked up his tools and
started to work. His back was bent and he was poor –
but now he was happy.

Retell the story

Encourage your child to retell the story in their own words using the pictures as prompts. You could do this together, or take it in turns. Have fun!

Once upon a time...

The end.

Practise Your Phonics With
Traditional Tales

More stories for you to enjoy...

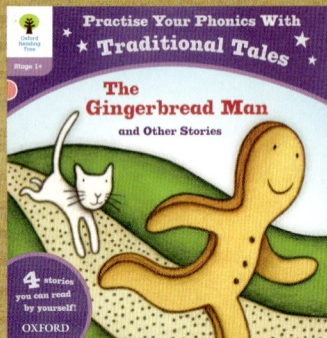

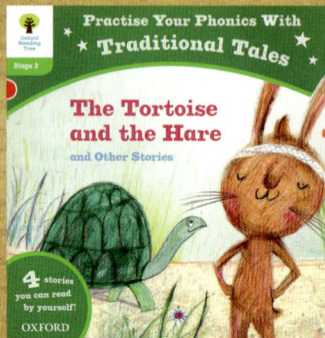

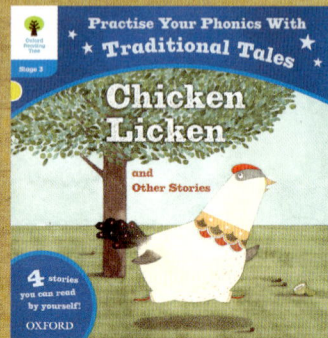

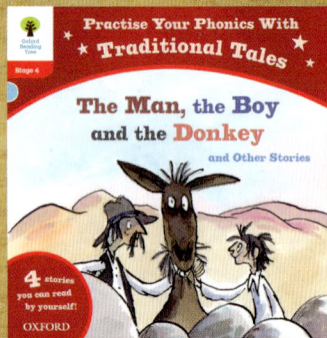

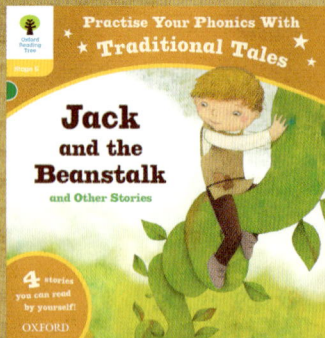

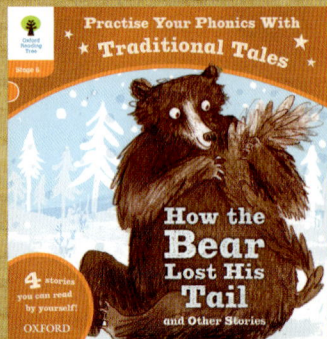

Practise Your Phonics With
Traditional Tales

Oxford Reading Tree
Stage 1+

The
Gingerbread Man
and Other Stories

4 stories you can read by yourself!
OXFORD

Practise Your Phonics With
Traditional Tales

Oxford Reading Tree
Stage 2

The Tortoise
and the Hare
and Other Stories

4 stories you can read by yourself!
OXFORD

Practise Your Phonics With
Traditional Tales

Oxford Reading Tree
Stage 3

Chicken
Licken
and Other Stories

4 stories you can read by yourself!
OXFORD

Practise Your Phonics With
Traditional Tales

Oxford Reading Tree
Stage 4

The Man, the Boy
and the **Donkey**
and Other Stories

4 stories you can read by yourself!
OXFORD

Practise Your Phonics With
Traditional Tales

Oxford Reading Tree
Stage 5

Jack
and the
Beanstalk
and Other Stories

4 stories you can read by yourself!
OXFORD

Practise Your Phonics With
Traditional Tales

Oxford Reading Tree
Stage 6

How the
Bear
Lost His
Tail
and Other Stories

4 stories you can read by yourself!
OXFORD

Help your child's learning with essential tips, phonics support and free eBooks

www.oxfordowl.co.uk

110